X

Town and County Government

IN THE

English Colonies of North America

"The common-law, in its grand simplicity, recognizing the right of all the rated parishioners to assemble in vestry, and administer parochial affairs."—*Sir T. Erskine May.*

"Parishes have municipal rights and duties which have existed and do exist, independent of any ecclesiastical organization."—*An Hereditary High Churchman.*

"The New England towns had no special originality, save the deep religious sentiment by which they were pervaded and controlled. They were naturally suggested by existing organizations, in England, substantially similar."—*Hon. Geo. F. Hoar.*

"It was of necessity, then, that the New Englander should provide a meeting house as soon as a church and town were organized. The edifice was called a meeting house; possibly at first because it was to be used indifferently as a place for both religious and civil transactions."—*President Noah Porter.*

"The vestries of that day represented all the local and municipal government there was in Virginia."—*Peyton's History of Augusta County.*

"Of course it became a parish and county at the same time."—*Bishop Meade.*

Town and County Government in the

ENGLISH COLONIES

OF NORTH AMERICA

Edward Channing, Ph.D.

HERITAGE BOOKS
2007

HERITAGE BOOKS

AN IMPRINT OF HERITAGE BOOKS, INC.

Books, CDs, and more—Worldwide

For our listing of thousands of titles see our website
at
www.HeritageBooks.com

A Facsimile Reprint
Published 2007 by
HERITAGE BOOKS, INC.
Publishing Division
65 East Main Street
Westminster, Maryland 21157-5026

Originally published

Baltimore
N. Murray, Publication Agent
John Hopkins University
October 1884

International Standard Book Number: 978-0-7884-4268-1

TOWN AND COUNTY GOVERNMENT

IN THE

ENGLISH COLONIES OF NORTH AMERICA.[1]

The Toppan Prize Essay for 1883.[2]

My researches in the Library of Harvard University have convinced me that the exact form which the local organization of each colony should assume depended on, (1) the economic conditions of the colony; (2) the experience in the management of local concerns which its founders brought from the mother-country; and (3) the form of church government and land system which should be found expedient.

---

[1] This line of research, a portion of the results of which are embodied in the following pages, was undertaken at the suggestion of Professor Henry W. Torrey, LL.D. This essay was written under the stimulus derived from Dr. H. B. Adams's paper on the Germanic Origin of New England Towns, Studies, First Series, II. Read before the Harvard Historical Society, May 9, 1881.—E. C.

[2] The Toppan Prize at Harvard is for the best essay on one of three subjects in Political Science. The essayist receives a prize of $150, the gift of Mr. R. N. Toppan, of the class of 1858. Competition is open to graduate students who have pursued a regular course of study at Harvard University during the year preceding the award of the prize, and also to undergraduate seniors. The Toppan Prize was first awarded in the year 1882 to Frank W. Taussig, Ph. D. (Harvard, 1883), Instructor in Political Economy at Harvard College, for a monograph on "Protection to Young Industries in the United States," published by Moses King, Cambridge, 1883; 2nd edition, by G. P. Putnam's Sons, New York, 1884. Dr. Channing's Prize Essay was read before the Historical and Political Science Association of the Johns Hopkins University, February 22, 1884, and also, in abstract, at the first meeting of the American Historical Association at Saratoga, in September, 1884.—ED.

ECONOMIC CONDITIONS.

As to the first of these historic factors we find that the physical conformation of New England, with the exception of what is now the State of Maine, necessitated settlement on the coast, and on the banks of the two rivers which penetrated the country; and necessitated, also, the spreading thence into the interior where the colonists "made their slow and painful way, much of it through the thick underbrush,—the husband with an axe on his shoulder, and what he can carry of household appendages in a pack on his back." Besides, neither the soil nor the climate were such as tempted men to live in scattered dwellings, or to cultivate large tracts of ground; and, in fine, the "nature and constitution of the place" were favorable to concentrated settlement for purposes of trading, fishing, and manufacturing, and not for an extended cultivation of the soil.

Turn to Virginia and we find a country cut into fragments by large navigable streams, forming harbors far in the interior, where the English ship could exchange her cargo of manufactured goods for tobacco grown in the vicinity. There, too, the climate was suited to a rural life, while a rich and almost inexhaustible soil was favorable to the growth of tobacco, the production of which, in the first years of the colony, was so profitable that it was grown in the streets of the only village which then existed; and so profitable that it was only by means of the most stringent laws, brutally enforced, that farmers could be compelled to grow enough food for themselves and their laborers. Where such conditions prevailed towns did not spring readily into being, nor could men be forced, bribed, or persuaded to live in them when founded.

To the south of Virginia somewhat similar economic conditions prevailed, especially in North Carolina; but in South Carolina, and to a greater extent in Georgia, we meet with large tracts of land difficult of access, and with a soil that produced no great staple like tobacco,—the cultivation of cotton in large quantities was not profitable until after the inventions of the cotton gin by Eli Whitney in 1792–. The climate of the upland portions of these colonies was suited to the shop, but that of the lowlands, while favorable to vegetation, was peculiarly fatal to the whites.

The physical formation of the middle colonies was favorable to either the town or county system of local government, and in each of them there grew up, in course of time, a great commercial town, the inhabitants of which seem to have differed materially in modes of thought and of life from the population of the surrounding districts, which was large, as both the soil and the climate were favorable to the extensive cultivation of breadstuffs.

LOCAL GOVERNMENT IN THE MOTHER COUNTRY.

The early settlers of New England belonged to the great middle class of old England, and they brought to their new home the ideas, energies, affections and hatreds of their ancestors. The early colonists of Virginia were purely English, but, while many of them belonged to the upper and middle classes of the mother country, there was, especially in early times, a large body of "servants," sprung from the lowest class of the English metropolis. After the introduction of negro slavery, this white slavery, for such it was, nominally went out of use; but the condition of the poor white, in colonial days, at least, was not much better than that of the white servant of an earlier date, or the negro slave of his own time. The result was that in Virginia the upper class took the reins of government into their hands at the start, and held them to the finish. In New England, on the contrary, the mass of the people, from the very earliest time, seized the control of affairs, fiercely resented any encroachment on what they considered their rights, and were the governing power when the Revolution burst upon them.[1] The institutions of the two colonies had a common origin, but so different has been their growth that their similarity can be discovered only after the most careful and exhaustive research.

The middle colonies were settled by a heterogeneous population: Dutch, Swedes, and English Puritans, Churchmen, Catholics, and Quakers, while the colonies to the south of Virginia were settled either as she herself had been, or by Scotch, Palatines, Huguenots, and English of all religions and degrees. The middle colonies gravitated towards the form of government that obtained in New England or Virginia, as proximity to one or the other dictated, while the local organization of the Carolinas was of a mixed character such as would naturally have been produced by the manner of their settlement. New England and Virginia dominated the continent, and it is to the political education of their founders that I now call attention. This education was acquired at the *town council*, the *county court*, and the *parish meeting*. The two first are well-known, but parish government in the early part of the seventeenth century, I believe, has never been satisfactorily explained; and, therefore, I will give the results

---

[1] There was an aristocracy in Massachusetts in 1775, as well as in Virginia. In the latter colony the aristocracy was the ruling class and upheld the cause of the colonists as against the crown, while in the former the aristocracy shared its political rights with the great mass of the people, and, when called upon to take one side or the other, went to Nova Scotia. Does not this desertion of the New England aristocracy, when coupled with the patriotic behavior of their peers in Virginia, account for the jealousy of Washington in certain quarters at the outset of the Revolution; and does it not also account for the fact that, of the first five presidents, four came from Virginia? It would also be interesting to inquire how much influence the fact that the New England aristocracy was an aristocracy of mere wealth—derived for the most part from mercantile pursuits, while that of Virginia was a landed aristocracy—may have had at the outbreak of the Revolution.

of my investigations which, it must be remembered, have been confined to the Library of Harvard University.[1]

The first thing that I wish to make clear is the meaning of the word parish as understood by the common and educated Englishman of 1600. For, whatever the true historical meaning of the word *parish* may be, it is reasonably certain that in England in 1600, it was used synonymously with *town*, and that it conveyed to the mind of the parish officer of that day very much the same idea as did the word town, that is, it was to him a territorial distinction. For instance, note the use of the two words in the following extract: " Memorandum that this year a thousand five hundred and eighty one by the consent of the *parish* of Stowmarket there was ground made to Thomas Kyrdersley and Thomas How of the ground commonly called the *town ground* of Stowmarket for the term of three years paying to the *churchwardens* . . . and the *town* further doth condition ; "[2] and also note the fact that the churchwardens of Kingston-on-Thames paid 6 d. " for bringing the town pot ;" and that, according to Toulmin Smith, " In country church-yards where there has never been any 'town,' in the modern sense, inscriptions will be found, both of old and recent date, naming the *parish, township*, or otherwise as the *town.*" So much for laymen, now let us see how the law writers of the time used the words.

---

[1] The best description of parish government in the olden time is Toulmin Smith's Parish ; but the book should be used with great caution as Mr. Smith is an enthusiast. I wish it to be understood that I am greatly indebted to this book, and I here give a general reference to it. But all the authorities cited in the text have been carefully examined by me, and have often been found to have been strangely twisted by Mr. Smith, an example of which is given on page 19 ; and, furthermore, a great many of these examples have been used by Mr. Smith and myself to elucidate different matters. The best description of the English parish at the present day is to be found in "The State and the Church," by the Hon. Arthur Elliot in The English Citizen Series.

[2] History of Stowmarket, p. 133.

William Lambard, writing in 1582, says: " The minister
or curate of the *parish*, and the constable, headborow or tith-
ingman of the *town* to which any popish recusant is sent shall
enter the name in a book to be kept in every parish for the
purpose."[1]   Sir Edward Coke in his description of "hue and
cry," given further on, always uses the word town, while Sir
Thomas Smith in describing the same thing invariably writes
parish ; while Coke in the "Institutes" speaks of "*towns* and
parishes within any shire, riding or *town corporate.*" Now,
what was a town or parish ?

The word for town in old law books is vill, thus " Chescun
burgh és un vill " is translated " every borough is a town."
Now as to the meaning of vill or town or parish, Lord Coke
says that " every place shall be called a vill if it does not
appear to the contrary, *but that it shall not be so accounted
where there is not and never was a* PAROCHIAL CHURCH."[2]   So
every parish should be intended to be but one vill, but nevertheless there might be more than one vill in a parish or more
than one parish in a vill.[3]   The following extract will, perhaps, show this point more clearly : " And all the judges in
the exchequer chamber over-ruled it to be good enough for
since it was first laid that trespass was done at *Hurley*, which
shall be understood a *town*, and then the defendant speaks of
the *parish aforesaid*, they shall be understood all one, and
two former judgments were cited accordingly for the word
aforesaid couples them."[4]   Sir John Fortescue says : " that
the boundaries of those vills are not ascertained by walls,
buildings or streets ; but by a compass of fields, large districts
of land," etc., and Selden, in commenting on the passage, says :

---

[1] Lambard, Constables, p. 68.

[2] Coke on Littleton, 115.

[3] Ibid., 125 ; Fleta, 4 c. 15, s. 9 ; Coke's Reports, V., 67 a ; Selden, de Dec.,
c. C. 53, p. 80.

[4] Hobart's Reports, 6. For additional cases of the use of the words by
lawyers. See Bulstrode's Rep., I., 60. See also Hobart's Rep., 41—Welsh
vs. Wray.

" It should seem that Villæ, Burgi, Civitates were, in our
Chancellor's [Fortescue] time confounded in use; nowadays
they are distinct : Vills being open, under the officers of the
crown as parts of the county, Boroughs are particular governments and corporations by prescription or charter." [1]

These extracts and others, for which there is no room here,
show that, in 1580–1640, town and parish were used both
by common and educated people as convertible terms, and
that a *town* was not a collection of houses, but was a division
of the county ; a certain parcel of land, the inhabitants of
which had certain duties to perform, and certain rights to
uphold, and that, as a rule, the inhabitants of one town per-
tained to one church, and were therefore parishioners ; and
that as the *town* and *parish* was commonly the same division
of land, so *parishioners*, and *townsmen* or *inhabitants* were
commonly the same persons ; and that town or parish was
used not only for a territorial distinction, but for the whole
body of the inhabitants of a town or parish, as for example :
" he consulted the parish," *i. e.*, the parishioners in parish
meeting assembled ; or " the town voted," for the townsmen [2]
in parish meeting, or vestry made a by-law.

The town or parish was responsible for the preservation of
the peace within its limits, for the maintenance of highways,
for the care of the poor, and for the proper transaction of all
business that was not manorial.   It had certain rights, the
most important of which was the granting or refusing money
for the reparation or alteration of the parish church.   It, also,
as a rule, had certain rights with regard to land, which, however, will not be considered in this place.

---

[1] Sir John Fortescue's De Laudibus Legum Angliæ, translated by John
Selden, 2d ed., 1741, p. 47 and note (F. 10) to the same.

[2] I use the word townsmen throughout this essay in its double meaning.
Here it is synonymous with parishioners or inhabitants.   Further on it
will be found used synonymously with selectmen.   I employ the word in
this manner in order to bring home the fact that it was so used by the New
England people themselves, a fact which has been sometimes doubted and
again proclaimed as a great discovery.

These functions were discharged through certain officers called parish officers (more properly town officers, for, as Canon Stubbs says, "there is primarily no connection between the parish and town"[1]); and by means of local ordinances or by-laws (local laws), which were made by a majority of the parishioners at a meeting called for the purpose.

This parish meeting, vestry, assembly of the parishioners or townsmen, was summoned by the parish officers; and seems to have been held in the nave of the church.[2] The summons was in the form of a notice, read in the church on Sunday, either before, during, or immediately after divine service, and proclaimed in the market-place[3]—if there was one—or posted at or near the church, and the meeting may even have been warned from door to door by the beadle. The exact form of the summons or warning was determined by local custom, but the notice in the church seems to have been necessary everywhere. To this meeting all those who had benefit of the things there transacted might come;[4] that is to say, all householders, and all who manured land within the parish. Such were technically termed inhabitants even though they dwelt in another town.[5]

The major part of such inhabitants, so assembled, could by their action, provided it was for the public good, bind all the inhabitants of the parish.[6] At these meetings business was transacted as the parishioners saw fit, although it seems to have been the custom, in many places, for the senior churchwarden to take the chair. The minutes of the meetings were kept by the churchwardens, or in some places, perhaps by a vestry clerk,—who must not be confounded with the clerk

---

[1] Stubbs' Const. Hist., I., 91.

[2] See page 28 for the same practice in Dorchester in early times.

[3] Jeffrey's Case in Coke's Repts., v. 66, 64.

[4] Strypes' Annals, Vol. I., 463.

[5] Coke Reports, v. 64, 66.

[6] Hobart, 212; Coke on Littleton, III. b; Cro. Jac. Rep., 498; Coke's Reports, V., 63, and note *a*; Salkeld Report, III., 76; Coke's Rep., XIII., 70.

of the parish — ; and usually, so far as rural parishes were concerned, they were signed by the churchwardens, the minister,
and by such of the parishioners as desired so to do. The
parson seems to have had no more share in these meetings
than his personal qualities might have given him; though,
undoubtedly, it was the custom in a very large number of
parishes for the parson to take the most prominent place long
before the Canons of 1603 attempted to give it him. These
parish meetings were held regularly for the receiving of
accounts (reckoning days, accompt days), and for the election
of parish officers. Besides these regular meetings there
were special meetings called to consent to the laying a rate
for the reparation of the church, the amendment of the highways, etc.

The parish officers were the constable, churchwardens,
swornmen, waymen, etc. As to the first of these William
Lambard says:[1] "The sundry names of constables or high
constables that be of Lathes, Rapes, Wapentakes, Hundreds
and Franchises, and the diverse names also of constables,
petie-constables, tythingmen, borsholders, boroheads, head-
borowes, chief-pledges, and such others if there be any that
bear office in towns, parishes, hamlets, tythings or borowes,
are all in effect but two: that is to say constables and Borsholders." And, "as constables were to the parishes and
towns, so were Borsholders to borowes and tythings."[2] The
constable of the hundred was called high constable " in com-
parison of the constable or petie-constable that be in towns or

---

[1] Lambard's Constables, ed. 1611, p. 4. William Lambard was born 1536,
and died 1601. The "Constables" was written in 1582, and the "Justice"
in 1581. He was a distinguished lawyer, and his "Constables" is a book
of the highest authority. See Bibliotheca Cantiana, by J. R. Smith and
Lambard's Perambulation of Kent, Ed. of 1826 Intro. (The edition of the
constables of 1611 is in the Law Library of Harvard University). For
constables, see also Comyn's Digest, and Sir Thomas Smith's Commonwealth of England, p. 89.

[2] Lambard's Constables, p. 11.

parishes within the hundred, whose part it likewise is to maintain the peace within the several limits of their own towns or parishes."[1]

The petty-constable, or constable as he was usually called, was by common-law elected at the leet or local criminal court by the jury or "hommage."[2] By prescription, however, he was often elected by the parishioners at their meetings. An old law writer gives this so quaintly that I am tempted to give his own words. He says, "where the custom of the place is for the jury in the leet to choose these officers, there they may and must be chosen still; for this is a good way and custom and the best way of choosing these officers; but where the custom is otherwise there it may be otherwise."[3]

It is impossible to ascertain the exact amount of authority possessed by the constable in 1600, but it is safe to say that it was less than in former times, although there is no doubt but that the ancient importance of the constable has been much exaggerated. It is possible that he once was the head man of the town or parish, and traces of this headship are to be found in the period under examination. As, for instance,[4] by the statute of Winchester the justices were to summon the constables or two of the most honest inhabitants of every town and parish and with their consent to tax." And the constables were consulted by the justices with regard to the state of the roads within their respective parishes, and as to other matters in respect to which their local knowledge was likely to be of

---

[1] Lambard's Constables, p. 5.

[2] Coke, Institutes, Part IV., 261, 262, 263 and 265, Works of Francis Bacon, edited by James Spedding, *et al.*, VIII., p. 70.

[3] William Sheppard, Offices and Duties of Constable, Borsholders, Tythingmen, etc., and other lay ministers whereunto are adjoyned the several offices of Church-ministers and Churchwardens, 1641, pages 12, 15, 17, 24. See also Lord Raymond's Reports, I., p. 74.

[4] Institutes of the laws of England by Sir Edward Coke, ed. of 1671, Part II, p. 697 and 704.

importance.[1] They, also, together with the churchwardens, summoned certain parish meetings, and took charge of the collecting and paying certain sums of money that each parish was required to contribute toward the relief of prisoners, maimed soldiers, etc.

The town or parish, as a territorial unit, was pecuniarily responsible for robberies and murders committed within its limits, unless the perpetrator was found, arrested, and delivered to the proper authority. The constable was, by common law, the police officer of the town or parish, and, as such, could take surety of the peace, cause hue and cry to be sent after an offender, and had charge of watch and ward.

The following is Coke's[2] description of hue and cry: " When any felony is committed, or any person grievously wounded, or any person assaulted, or offered to be robbed either in the day or night; the party grieved or any other may resort to the constable of the town, . . . , and require him to raise hue and cry. And the duty of the constable is to raise the power of the town, as well in the night as in the day, for the prosecution of the offender, and if he be not found there to give the next constable warning," etc. This system worked well, for, as Sir Thomas Smith[3] says: " This hue and crie from parish to parish is carried, till the thiefe or robber be found. That parish which doth not his duty, but letteth by their negligence the thiefe to depart, doth not only pay a fine to the King, but must repay the partie robbed his damages. So that every English man is a *sergeant* to take the thiefe, and who sheweth himself negligent therein."

In every town a watch was posted at night, in some convenient place to see what suspicious persons " do walk in the night," and if such were found they were stopped and examined. If there was any especial reason for it, wardsmen were

[1] Sheppard, 124 and 193. Lambard, p. 36.
[2] Institutes, pt. 3, p. 116.
[3] Commonwealth of England, p. 86.

appointed by day to arrest " Roberdsmen, drawlatches and wasters."[1] In fine, the constable had charge of the police of the parish, and in addition gave the benefit of his local knowledge to the county authorities.

In early times the churchwarden was a temporal officer ; at the present time his office is spiritual, and it is very difficult to discover what his exact status in 1600 was. Lambard says that he " was put in trust for the behoof of the parishioners,"[2] while Sheppard calls him a spiritual officer.[3] Coke in reporting a case decided in 1610, while describing the office of parish clerk, says: " this office is like unto the office of churchwarden, who although they be chosen for two years yet for cause they, the parishioners, may displace them as is holden in 26 H. VIII. 5, *and although the office concerneth divine service—yet the office itself is temporal.*"[4]

The election of churchwardens was " by common right," in the parishioners,[5] but it is reasonably certain, that, in 1600, it was the custom in a very large number of places for the parson to have a voice in their election, and it is possible that he may, even at that time, have appointed one himself. As a rule there were two churchwardens in each parish, but some large undivided parishes had three, and in parishes comprising a number of townships, villages, hamlets, etc., one or more

[1] Sheppard, p. 37.
[2] Lambard, 72 (1582).
[3] Sheppard, 314 (1641).
[4] Coke's Reports, XIII., 70.
The following bonde is extracted from the records of Stowmarket (Hist. Stowmarket, 134). " 9 Jan. 1576. We appoint churchwardens for the yeare ensuing John Scarlet, John Revet to provide all these foresaid duties owing to ye towne—and to make a true reckning thereof at the end of there yeare —to make in this office a faithful inventory to ye towne—to yield a true accompt at the next reckning day, and then deliver such sums of money as are due to the towne in the parishes, and remain in the Hundred—and this to do they bind themselves singly and severallie to ye towne by their handes hereto subscribed."
[5] Cro. Jac. 553 and 532 ; Coke's Rep., II., 38 ; Sheppard, 314 ; Salk., III., 90.

wardens was elected for each such sub-division. Their term of office was, *usually*, annual, and they were sworn and admitted by the archdeacon, who, however, could not refuse them.[1]

The churchwardens, in common law, were "taken as a manner of corporation," says Lambard.[2] And as such, they were to bring all actions at law, stating, however, that the loss or breach complained of was, " *ad damnum parochianorum.*" They had charge of the ornaments, vestments, etc., which were used in the conduct of divine service, (all of which belonged to the parishioners and not to the parson), and they were intrusted with the care of the church fabric—including the tower and bells—but not the chancel. They had no property in these things and were required to account for them when their term of office was over.

They were to observe the manners of the parson and parishioners, and to report any misconduct on the part of either, to the Ordinary at Visitation. The churchwardens *ex officio*, and four, three, or two of every parish, chosen by the parishioners thereof, and appointed by the justices of the peace, were overseers of the poor;[3] and were to raise "weekly or otherwise by taxation of every inhabitant, parson, vicar and others, and of every occupier of lands, houses, tithes impropriate [etc.] in the said parish" the funds required for the carrying into effect the poor law of Elizabeth.[4] The parish was obliged to pay the sum required by these overseers, who, however, often consulted the parishioners before deciding as to the amount; and the *manner* of raising it was by "agreement of the parishioners within themselves." This poor-rate was not necessarily borne equally by the ratepayers, "for if a parishioner . . . shall bring into the parish without the consent thereof, a stranger who is, or is

---

[1] Sheppard, 516.
[2] Lambard, 70; see also Salk., Repts, III., p. 90.
[3] Lambard, 77.
[4] Lambard, 38; Sheppard, 226.

2

apparently like to be burthensome, in this case the parishioners . . . may rate him, not only according to his ability
of lands and goods, but according to the damage he bringeth
or is like to bring to the parish by his folly."[1] The overseers had the disposal of the sums so raised, but were required
to exhibit their accounts to the parishioners at certain stated
times, and could call parish meetings on the "poor's business."

The churchwardens and the constable were "yearly to call
together a number of the parishioners, and to choose two
honest men of their parish to be surveyors of the works for
the amendment of the highways, . . . , and ought also then
to appoint six days for the amendment of those highways."
But the most important duty of the churchwarden in 1600
was the care of the church fabric and of the things connected
with divine service. Whatever money was necessary for this
purpose was raised by a tax called the church-rate. This
rate[2] could be made only after the necessity for the money
had actually arisen, and then such rate was not good unless
made before and with the consent of the major part of the
parishioners assembled after due warning. The wardens had
the collecting and disbursing of this money—unless collectors
were appointed—but they were obliged to account to the
parishioners at regular intervals.[3]

A body of men—synodsmen, questmen, sidesmen, or swornmen—was well known to the writers of Queen Elizabeth's
time,[4] and to those who drew up the Canons of 1641, but it is
very difficult to discover any thing concerning them. The
following extracts are almost the only thing that I have
found. The first is from Strype's Annals,[5] under date of
1564: "To every parish belongeth . . . .; V. four or eight

[1] Sheppard, 232.
[2] Sheppard, 327.
[3] Sheppard, 332.
[4] Calendar of State Papers, Dom. 1519–1594, p. 158; Ib., 1598–1601, p. 171 and 519; Ib., 1547–1565, p. 141.
[5] 2d ed. 1725, Vol. I., p. 463.

jurats for offences given and taken. [These seem to be a
kind of censors or spies upon the manners of the people]
. . . .; VII. An assistance, being thirteen persons, to con-
sist of such only as had before been churchwardens and constables." The words in brackets are bracketed in the origi-
nal, Toulmin Smith leaves them out, translates the word
jurat—swornmen, and on the authority of the extract so
explained, says that there was in each parish a committee of
arbitration — like the arbitrators of Providence or the peace-
makers of Pennsylvania — all of which may be true enough,
but is not borne out by Strype. As to assistance Mr. Smith
says, that the old designation of the governing body of many
old corporations was " Court of Assistants," and further that
there was a committee of assistance in every parish, and that
it developed into the *select vestry.* If this last is true, and
there is no reason, so far as I know, to doubt it, the origin
of the New England selectmen and of the Virginia vestry is
perfectly clear.

Sheppard, writing in 1640, describes sidesmen as follows:
" The sidesmen or Questmen are those that are yearly chosen
. . . . to assist the churchwardens in their inquiry and pre-
sentment of such offenders to the ordinary as are punishable
in the Christian court. And herein it seems the course is at
this day in some places to choose and swear the old churchwardens to this office, for when the new churchwardens are
sworn, and the old discharged, the course is to swear the old
churchwardens to be aiding and assisting to the new churchwardens: and in other places they choose *others amongst the*
meaner sort of the people. And these officers also by the
canon are to be chosen and made yearly in the Easter week
by the minister and the parishioners, ... they are . . . .
to present the misdemeanors of the parishioners as far forth
as the churchwardens." This seems to be a description of the
jurats and assistance combined. The 21 Jac. I., c. 12 men-

---

[1]Sheppard, 117.

tions "churchwardens, and all persons called swornmen executing the office of churchwardens." And finally Archbishop Gibson says that sidesmen and assistants are the same.[1]

From these extracts it will be seen that almost nothing is known of the office, and that even its name is strangely given. But, it seems to me that jurats, questmen, swornmen, sidesmen, synodsmen, and assistants were all one, and that there did exist in many parishes a body of men, elected as the churchwardens were, and consisting of such old wardens, constables, and other honest freeholders as the parishioners saw fit; that this body acted as an advisory board to the parish or town officers; that it developed into the select vestry of later times; and that it is the only institution which offers a suggestion as to the origin of the prudential men, townsmen, ten men or selectmen of early New England.

The waymen,[2] waywardens, surveyors, supervisors or overseers of the highways, were two in number, and were yearly chosen to that office by the parishioners at a meeting called for the purpose by the constable and churchwardens. In 1600 their duties were those of mere foremen. At that time the parish was responsible for the condition of the highways and, generally, of the bridges within its limits. Whatever money was needed to purchase material to keep roads and bridges in repair was raised by the highway rate, a rate assessed and collected as the parish saw fit.

The labor was provided in this way. The constables and churchwardens appointed six days in each year for working on the roads, and gave due notice of those days in the church. "And this being done these officers, viz., the surveyors of the highways are to see that the same be observed, and that all the parishioners do their work on the same days in manner as followeth, Every person having a plough land in tillage or in

[1] This is on the authority of Smith, as I have been unable to get hold of a copy of Gibson on Visitation.

[2] Lambard, 36; Sheppard, 193; Statute 2 and 3, P. and M. chap. 8 (1585).

pasture in the same parish or keeping there a plough or a draught, shall find and send on every day to the place designated one wain or cart, provided after the fashion of the country with oxen, etc. fit for the carriage, and with necessary tools fit for the work, and with two able men ; and then and there these men must do such work with their plow, etc. as they shall be appointed to do by the surveyors aforesaid, by the space of eight hours on every of the said days under pain to forfeit for every default ten shillings. And every householder, cottager and laborer of the parish (able to labor and having *no paid servant by the year*) must by himself or some other able man be then and there ready to work, and work," etc.

The other officers of the parish were the *parish clerk* who was the parson's assistant and whose duty was to " read, write, sing, and say." The office was temporal and the officer was elected after the manner of electing churchwardens.[1] The *vestry clerk* was the secretary of the parishioners, although the records were usually kept by the wardens or the minister. When a clerk was required, however, he was elected by the parishioners for one meeting or longer ; and his duty was to keep the vestry minute book, which was the record of the doings of the parishioners (townsmen) and of the parish officers (town officers), as distinguished from the parish register or record of births, deaths, and marriages.

The beadle was the ministerial officer of the parish, and executed the orders of the parish officers, and besides did duty as a police officer. The words hayward (hedgewardens), impounders — of cattle —, common driver — of cattle —, are often found in the old records and explain themselves.

In the second part of this essay I shall describe the government of some of the colonies, and contrast a few of the institutions there existing with these institutions of England in 1600.

---

[1] Cro. Jac., 370; 21, James I, in B. R.

ECCLESIASTICAL SYSTEMS IN THE COLONIES.

" The New England Meeting House is the symbol of much that is characteristic of New England life. Its erection was the starting point of every one of the earlier New England communities, and it has been the rallying point of everything that is distinctive in their history." These words of one of the keenest observers[1] of our early institutions will apply equally well to Virginia if we substitute church for meeting house; for the Virginia parish (in many cases identical with the county), with its vestry and churchwardens, was there the starting point of all social intercourse and of all government. With the meeting house is associated puritanism and congregationalism; with the vestry, episcopacy.

Now, congregationalism was a form of church government, and, where combined as here with puritanism, was a form of social government also. The peculiar social features of that system necessitated the settlement of a puritan colony by communities. It is to these facts, rather than to any especial religious belief, that the influence of puritanism is to be traced.

The puritans who settled at the " Bay " must not be confounded with the Pilgrims who founded Plymouth. The latter were *separatists* from the English church, while the former belonged to the Church of England, not what we now know by that name, but to the great body of Christian believers in England. Their desire was to purify the religious and social life of that church, but not to leave it. After they arrived on this side of the water they were obliged to adopt another form of church government, and, once started in the opposite direction from that taken by Laud, there was no returning. But I believe in the sincerity of their assertions on leaving England, and I believe their growth apart from the English church was much slower than is generally thought.

---

[1] President Porter.

As to Virginia, the upper class belonged to the Cavaliers and the lower class had not as yet learned to think for themselves. The result was that the " Anglican " form was introduced into Virginia as soon as it was in England, and the soil being more congenial, this form developed without the struggles which it encountered in the mother country. In Virginia, as in old England, it was because the social features of the church system were suited to the life of the people that the Episcopalian form was adopted, and that, when once introduced, it intensified the action of the other factors above enumerated.

There are some striking similarities between the ecclesiastical systems of the two colonies that deserve a brief mention. In Massachusetts and Virginia, the ruling body of the various ecclesiastical organizations seized and held the right of choosing the minister. In Virginia it was the vestry which claimed to be the patron in as much as it provided the parson with house, glebe, and church; while in Massachusetts the congregation exercised the same power for essentially the same reason. In both colonies the temporal power gave an expressed or implied consent to the appointment.

Another similarity is the fact that the Episcopalians in Virginia and the Puritans at the " Bay," claimed and exercised the right of turning out whosoever should disturb them in their religious beliefs, and here again for essentially the same reason, namely, because it was the only way that a quiet and profitable existence could be secured. In both colonies the county court took the place of the Visitation. The ecclesiastical forms prevailing in the other colonies were such as were suited to the heterogeneous forms of local government there existing. Antinomianism and Quakerism were but a few steps removed from Puritanism, while the Catholicism of Maryland and Virginia was different in creed and discipline, rather than in social features.

Land Systems.

In New England,[1] in the early days, there were large tracts of land granted to individuals, who had either adventured considerable sums of money or performed important services for the colony. But these large grants were exceptional and the policy of the rulers was to give land to such persons only as could and would found a town and gather a church. To be sure, at the first settlement, towns grew up without any such formal authorization, but after 1640 no one was permitted to settle on the vacant land within the chartered limits without permission. The General Court adopted then the system of granting lands in townships to seven or more individuals who had, as a rule, the absolute disposal of the land so obtained. Sometimes these grantees resigned their rights in favor of the town; sometimes they divided the land between themselves and such others as they chose to admit to a partnership; and thus in many cases there grew up in a town two " bodies "—so-called—one the town proper, which conducted its business through the town meeting in which, at first, any person inhabiting within the town had a vote. This right was afterwards restricted to church-members, and, at a still later date, could be exercised by those only who possessed a certain amount of property. The other body was composed of the proprietors of the undivided land who transacted their business in a meeting at which the townsman, as such, had no vote. The point, however, so far as we are concerned in this place, is that the land was not given to individuals, but to groups of persons who desired to live and worship together.

---

[1] The best account of the land system of New England is by Melville Egleston, " Land Systems of New England." Unfortunately the essay was privately printed. See also "The Records of Groton," by S. A. Green, especially the introduction to the second part.

In Virginia[1] land was granted to individuals from beginning to end, and the early grants were of such great extent that certain portions of the country were said to be "cantonized by grants to particular persons."

After the dissolution of the "Company" fifty acres were given to any one who should "adventure into that country" or who should pay the cost of another person's coming. This "fifty acres" was called a "right," and great frauds were perpetrated in the giving and surveying of these "rights." The grantee agreed to "seat" within three years after date and to pay a quitrent. The quitrents were easily evaded and the "seating" was a mere form. Thus all the details of the Virginia land system seem to have been devised to secure the largest amount of land to the smallest number of persons:[2] that is, diametrically opposed to the system that prevailed in New England.

In the other colonies, no system can be traced, except perhaps in New York, where the feudal nature of the early grants is well known. I have been unable to make anything out of the material at my command with regard to Pennsylvania, and I was gratified to find that the best authority[3] on the subject had met with a similar difficulty; and what he says is true not only of Pennsylvania but of North and South Carolina and to a great extent of New York. Judge Smith, in the course of a long note, writes:[4] "Whatever uniform plan of settling the country and conveying his lands the first

---

[1] In Neill's "Virginia Company" will be found much information scattered through the volume, which has a good index. See also "The Present State of Virginia," by Blair, Hartwell, and Chilton; and Beverley, *passim.*

[2] John Bolling, who died in 1757, left an estate of 40,000 acres, and this is not mentioned as an extraordinary amount of land for one man to own. Slaughter, History of Bristol Parish, p. 10.

[3] Judge William Smith.

[4] Laws of Pennsylvania, Ed. 1810, Vol. II., 137. Cited as Smith's Laws, or more commonly as Dallas', Vol. II., 137, 140, 141; see also History of Delaware County by George Smith; and "Breviate," page 56.

proprietor may have contemplated or devised, it must very early have been found impracticable on experience. At present no regular system can be traced upon the public records. The terms of sale were changed from time to time; and as the affairs of the Land-office were not familiar to the mass of the people it is not to be wondered at, that the assembly, even in the year 1755, in an address to Governor Morris, declare, 'that the state and management of the Land-office is pretty much of a mystery.'"

Thus we find that, in Massachusetts and Virginia, certain causes, so called, were well marked. The economic conditions, the ecclesiastical system, and the manner of granting lands were radically different, but, in each case, were so combined as to produce a strong and healthy growth, while the previous political training of the rulers was essentially the same. As to the other colonies the conditions were so various and combined in such a multitude of ways, that to describe properly their early constitutional history and their local governments would require very much more space than can here be given. And after all, sooner or later the Massachusetts town, or the Virginia parish and county, has been introduced into every one of them. I shall first consider the town, its early history and development, and its perfected form; then the county will be discussed, and finally the two systems will be compared with one another and with their great prototype, the *parish*.

LOCAL GOVERNMENT IN MASSACHUSETTS.[1]

The towns of Massachusetts Bay may be divided into two classes: those which were settled without any formal authorization from the Company, Dorchester for example, and those,

---

[1] On the early history of local institutions, see Professor Joel Parker's paper on the Towns of New England (Mass. Hist. Soc. Proc., Vol. for 1866–67, pp. 14–65), in which he lays down the doctrine—directly opposed to

like Woburn, which were founded only after express permission had been obtained. First as to Dorchester. " In the year of our Lord, 1629, divers godly persons from Devonshire, Somersetshire, Dorsetshire and other places "[1] assembled at Plymouth, England, and "resolved to live together; and therefore as they had made choice of those two Rev. servants of God, Mr. John Warham and Mr. John Maverick to be their ministers, so they kept a solemn day of fasting, ... ; and in the latter part of the day, as the people did solemnly make choice of, and call those godly ministers to be their *Officers,* so also the Rev. Mr. Warham and Mr. Maverick did accept thereof and expressed the same."[2]

---

that maintained in this essay—that those towns "were not founded or modelled on precedent;" but grew, as he maintained in the Jaffrey Oration delivered in 1873, "out of the democratic principle of self-government." This system—he further maintained in the same oration—which "was inaugurated at Plymouth, commended itself to the Massachusetts Colony so that it was adopted there at the outset.'" It is unpleasant to be obliged to differ from so high an authority, but I do not believe that Plymouth exercised so much influence on the early institutions of Massachusetts as Professor Parker asserted. And, without arguing the question, it may be well to point out that the deference paid to the Pilgrims two hundred and fifty years ago was much less than now, or, to use a bold figure of speech, Plymouth Rock had not then attained the enormous proportions it has since assumed.

In 1870—that is, between Professor Parker's two essays—Mr. Richard Frothingham read a paper before the American Antiquarian Society (Proceedings for Oct., 1870), in which he gave the results of an examination of the early laws of several of the English colonies, which results were widely different from those of Professor Parker, and which gave rise to the remark of Senator Hoar to be found among the mottoes of this paper.

The next scholar to study this question with much care was Dr. H. B. Adams, whose papers are in the first volume of the present publication, and whose conclusions are corroborated by those arrived at here. Another essay which has been of great service to me is President Porter's paper on the New England Meeting House (New Englander, May, 1883), which is certainly not opposed to the theory here laid down.

[1] Collections of the Dorchester Antiquarian and Historical Society, No. 1, Blake's Annals, p. 7.

[2] Roger Clap's Memoirs, p. 39, in the same volume as the above.

Soon after they set sail, and on the 30th May, 1630, they landed "in health" at Nantasket. After a brief exploration of the country they decided to settle "at a place called Mattapan" (Dorchester Neck), "because there was a Neck of Land fit to keep our cattle on." In a short time Winthrop and the rest arrived and settled at various places in the vicinity.

The first entry in the Dorchester Town Records is under the date of 1632, and the intervening years had been passed "in working themselves into settlements, and incorporating into a body to carry on the public affairs of the plantation; in granting many parcels of land and meadow to, I suppose every particular person."[1] The first entries in the record book relate to the allotment of land and the erection of fences; but on Monday, the eighth of October, 1633, by the whole consent of the plantation it was agreed and ordered for the general good of the *plantation,* that on certain days, in the morning, "and presently upon the *beating of the drum* there should be a *general meeting* of the inhabitants of the plantation at the *meeting house,* there to settle (and set down) such orders as may tend to the general good as aforesaid, and every man to be bound thereby without gainsaying or resistance," and "that twelve men" should be selected out of the "company" who should name the ordering of all things "until the next monthly meeting, and afterwards if it be not contradicted and otherwise ordered."[2] The number of these men and the term of their office was altered from time to time, and their authority was in some ways diminished, in others enlarged, and completely ascertained and defined; but this order was, in reality, the beginning of the town government of Dorchester, so far as any records that have come down to us show.

---

[1] Blake's Annals, p. 11.

[2] Fourth Report of the Record Commissioners of Boston; Records of the Town of Dorchester, p. 3.

All the orders in those records before September, 1634, were signed by John Maverick, John Warham, Will. Gaylord, Will. Rockwell, or any two or three of them. The first two were the ministers, and the others I have seen somewhere[1] described as deacons. In 1637 an order was signed by twenty men who appear to have been the selectmen for that year. In 1636 a "bayliff" was chosen to levy "all fines, rates and amercements for the plantation;" a mode of land registration was devised; and assessors or raters, and other officers were appointed.

So much for the early history of Dorchester. I will only add that the word "town" occurs for the first time in these records under date of February 1640 (O. S.) and that in 1642 "town-meeting" appears; and that in 1644-5 the record is "Witnessed By John Wiswell beinge moderator of 7 men George Weeks," which entry, by the way, stands immediately before the first mention of selectmen. And now, let us examine the records[2] of the Massachusetts Bay Company, and see what therein concerns towns and counties.

The first order concerning the allotment of lands relates to New England's Plantation (Salem). One of the last clauses provides that if an allotment should not be made within ten days after the arrival of an adventurer, in the colony, then he or his servant could settle at any convenient spot.[3] This order was passed at a court of assistants held the 21st of May, 1629. August 26 of that year witnessed the "Agreement at Cambridge,"[4] and a few days later it was decided to transfer[5]

---

[1] History of Dorchester by a Committee of the Dorchester Hist. and Antiq. Soc.

[2] In the Records of the Massachusetts Bay Company cited as Company's Records, under date Apr. 30th, 1629, will be found the form of government adopted for this plantation. *This order* concerning lands is under date 19 May, 1629, Vol. I., 43, 44. Melville Egleston, Land Systems, p. 14.

[3] Company's Records, Vol. I., p. 363.

[4] Hutchinson's Collections, p. 25.

[5] Company's Records, I., 51.

the charter, and with it the government of the colony to New England. What further agreements there may have been between the various interested parties concerning the allotment of lands and the form of government to be adopted, or how these questions were settled, is now a matter of mere conjecture.[1] The order above referred to may have been extended or a new order may have been adopted. All we know is that the settlers of Dorchester, and after them the founders of Charlestown, Watertown, and Boston, settled on sites of their own choosing, allotted lands in severalty, and, in fine, appear to have considered themselves as much entitled to their lands before any grant whatever was made by the General Court, on this side the water, as they did after that time.

At one of the first meetings it was ordered " That Trimountain shall be called Boston, Mattapan Dorchester,"[2] etc.; and all persons were warned against settling within the Company's limit without leave. At a Court of Assistants held shortly after, John Woodberry was chosen constable for Dorchester, and at that meeting, or at the next General Court, constables were chosen for the other places, and this continued to be the way of appointing them for some time, but what that officer's duties were in early times does not appear.[3]

On the first of April, 1634, the following order was passed, namely, " that the constable and four more of the chief inhabitants of every town, (to be chosen by the freemen there,) with the advice of some one or more of the assistants,"[4] shall

---

[1] Melville Egleston, Land Systems of New England, p. 24.

[2] The Records of the Company of Massachusetts Bay are generally called Colonial Records after this date, but I shall continue to cite them as before, Company's Records, I., 75.

[3] See however "Norman Constables in America," Studies, First Series, VIII, by H. B. Adams, Ph. D. The duties of constables as described by Dr. Adams apply to an England of a time not considered by me, and also to the constables of Plymouth and Salem, both of which towns had an anomalous form of government in the early times. See also on this point Company's Records, II., pt. 1, p. 324.

[4] Company's Records, I., 116.

make a survey of the " lands of every free inhabitant there
and enter the same on a book," a copy of which was to be
given to the General Court. All sales and grants in the
future were to be dealt with in the same way, and " this
assurance of lands," as it was called, was extended the next
year to such as were not freemen, but had taken their oaths
respectively.[1] At the meeting of the General Court held the
14th May, 1634, the representative system[2] was introduced,
the plantation or town being adopted as the basis. The jury
system was introduced, and taxes were to be in the future
levied on real and personal estate and not " according to the
number of his persons."[3]

The General Court at the same time that it passed the order
for a standing council, devised a system for the future
settlement of plantations. It declared " that the major part
of the magistrates shall have power, . . . to dispose of the
sitting down of men in any new plantation, and that none
shall go without leave from them,"[4] and " that such as shall
build houses in any town liberties prejudicial to the town,
without leave from the town, the inhabitants of the said town
shall have power to demolish the said houses, and remove the
persons.[5] And it was declared that for the future the General
Court would not recognize any church, unless such had been
gathered with the approbation of the magistrates and the
elders of a majority of the churches within the colony, and
that the members of such churches only should hereafter be
admitted to the freedom of the " *commonwealth.*"[6]

In March, 1635, it was ordered that as " the particular
towns have many things which concern only themselves, and

[1] Company's Records, Vol. I., p. 137.
[2] Company's Records, Vol. I., p. 118.
[3] Company's Records, Vol. I., p. 120.
[4] Melville Egleston, Land Systems; Company's Records, Vol. I., p. 167.
[5] Company's Records, Vol. I., p. 168.
[6] Company's Records, Vol. I., p. 168.

the ordering of their own affairs, and the disposing of business in their own town" that the "freeman of every town shall only have power to dispose of their own lands and woods with all the privileges and appurtenances of the said town to grant lots and make such orders as may concern the well ordering of their own towns, not repugnant to the laws and orders as have been established by the General Court, as also to lay mulcts and penalties to the breach of these orders, and to lay and distrain the same not to exceed the sum of 20 shillings also to choose their own particular officers."[1]   By this law it will be noticed that none but freemen had any voice in the local government, but in 1647, non-freemen who had taken the oath of fidelity were admitted to a share in the carrying on of the town affairs.[2]   With regard to this matter of voting in town meeting, it must be borne in mind, as I have above indicated, that, in the towns founded after the order of 1634, those who had a voice in the conduct of the prudential and other affairs did not necessarily have a voice in the allotment of lands.[3]   A little later it was agreed that the order of the court "against the building of dwelling houses above half a mile from the meeting house shall extend to all the towns in this jurisdiction."[4]   In 1638 a committee was appointed to report to the next meeting as to a method of granting land,[5] thus showing that the rulers of the colony were anxious that the settlements should not be too much scattered.   In the same year every inhabitant of a town was declared liable for his proportion of the town's charges, both in church and commonwealth.[6]

---

[1] Company's Records, Vol. I., p. 172.
[2] Company's Records, Vol. II., p. 197; compare *post*, page 37.
[3] Records of the Town of Groton, by S. A. Green, p. 133, *et seq.*; and Melville Egleston as above.
[4] Company's Records, I., 181.
[5] Company's Records, I., 240.
[6] Company's Records, I., 240.

In 1639, Winnaconnet was "allowed" to be a town, with
power to chose a constable and other officers, to make orders
for the well ordering of the town, to send a deputy to the
General Court, and to be called Hampton.[1] This brings us
to the founding of Woburn which was as follows.

In 1640[2] news was brought to Charlestown of the con-
veniency of land thereto adjoining. A petition was sent to
the General Court, which was granted in the following
terms: "Charlestown was granted their petition, that is two
miles at their head line, provided it fall not within the
bounds of Lynn village, and that they build within two
years."[3] Six men, Edward Johnson among them, were
chosen by the Charlestown people to regulate the settling of
this new plantation,[4] and they seem to have had little trouble
in so doing; for by 1644 the "village" had grown to such
an extent that provisions for a regular town government
were made; "according to the liberties and privileges granted
to the several towns in this jurisdiction." The following are
a few extracts from that "Body of Liberties"[5] which very
well show the power of a town at that early day: "The freemen of every township shall have power to make such by-laws
and constitutions as may concern the welfare of their town,
provided that they be not of a criminal, but only of a prudential nature, and that their penalties exceed not 20s. for
one offence, and that they be not repugnant to the public
laws and orders of the countrie,"[6] etc. "It is the liberty of
the freemen to choose such deputies for the General Court,"[7]
etc. "The freemen of every town or township, shall have

---

[1] Company's Records, Vol. I., 259.
[2] Woburn Town Records in Poole's Introduction to Wonder Working
Providence.
[3] Company's Records, Vol. I., 290.
[4] Wonder Working Providence, 175.
[5] Mass. Hist. Soc. Coll. XXVIII., 3rd Series, Vol. 8, pp. 216–237.
[6] Ibid., p. 227, sec. 66.
[7] Body of Liberties, as above, p. 227, sec. 68.

full power to choose yearly or for less time out of themselves
a convenient number of fit men to order the planting or prudential occasions of that town, according to instructions given
them in writing, provided nothing be done by them contrary
to the public laws and orders of the country, provided also
the number of such SELECT PERSONS be not above nine."[1]

Such was the origin of town government in Massachusetts
Bay. Let us now turn over the records and see when the
county came into existence. In March, 1635-36, the General
Court ordered that there should be four courts kept every
quarter at each of the following places: "1, at Ipswich, to
which Newberry shall belong; 2, at Salem, to which Saugus
shall belong; 3, at New Town, to which Charlestown, Concord, Medford and Watertown shall belong; 4, at Boston, to
which Roxbury, Dorchester, Weymouth and Hingham shall
belong."[2] These courts, which were to be held by any of
the magistrates who happened to dwell near the court town,
and by such others as the General Court should choose out of
a greater number to be nominated by the several towns, had
jurisdiction in all civil causes under £10, and in criminal
matters not concerning life, limb or banishment. "All
actions shall be tried at that court to which the defendant
belongs, and an appeal be laid to the Quarter Court."

In 1636 the military men were divided into three regi-
ments, those of Boston, Dorchester, Roxbury, Weymouth,
and Hingham forming one; those of Charlestown, Newtown,
Watertown, Concord, and Dedham to be another; and those
of Saugus, Salem and Newberry to be the third.[3]

In 1643 the whole colony, which then included all of the
present state of New Hampshire that was then settled, was
divided into four "*shires:*"[4] Essex, Middlesex, Suffolk and

---

[1] Ibid., p. 228, sec. 74.
[2] Company Records, Vol. I., p. 169.
[3] Company's Records, Vol. I., p. 186.
[4] Company's Records, Vol. II., p. 38.

Norfolk. Suffolk included the towns of Boston, Roxbury, Dorchester, Dedham, Weymouth, Hingham, and Nantasket—about the same territory as was included in the jurisdiction of Court No. 4, of 1636, and which formed the first regiment of the same year. Norfolk was composed of Salisbury, Hampton, Haverhill, Exeter, Dover, and Strawberry Bank (Portsmouth). Essex included the territory now known by that name, and Middlesex was composed of the towns above mentioned as belonging to Court No. 3.

At the next session of the General Court the militia was reorganized.[1] In the new arrangement each "town was a company," and the companies of each shire formed a regiment. For every shire a lieutenant was to have been appointed, whose duty it was, so far as I can find, to call out the militia in case of need, and to consult with the governor, the commander in chief, and the sergeant major, who seems to have had the real command of the regiment. As may be seen, it is very difficult to discern in what need the county arose, whether for judicial purposes, as Prof. Washburn[2] maintained, or for a better military organization, as Edward Johnson[3] hinted, or from the need of some such officer as the sheriff.

The other territorial distinctions were plantation, village, township, district, precinct, and parish. Plantation seems to have been used, in the early time, for the whole colony, for a town, or more technically, perhaps, for a community which had not acquired the dignity of a town. Village was used to designate a plantation made by a town as Charlestown Village (Woburn), or Lynn Village (Saugus). Township, at first, meant merely a tract of land granted to persons who intended there to settle a town and gather a church. At a later day it was used almost synonymously with town, thus

---

[1] Company's Records, II., 42.
[2] Judicial History of Massachusetts, p. 31, Note 1.
[3] Wonder Working Providence, p. 191.

".... shall be a township and be called by the name of Attleborough, and shall have and enjoy all such immunities, privileges, and powers as generally *other towns* within this province," etc.

As to the last three of these terms, viz.: district, precinct, and parish, it is impossible to form an intelligent opinion, but Mr. Buck[1] seems to have stated the matter correctly when he wrote: that " our convenient distinction between town and parish was little known, town, precinct, parish and district, were terms indiscriminately used [in 'Province Laws'] for ecclesiastical and civil purposes."

The town, the inhabitants of which belonged to one church, was the political unit in Massachusetts. The way in which the words town and church were used may be seen in the following extract: " Dorchester was the first settled church and town in Massachusetts." So long as the greater number of dwelling houses in the town were within half a mile of the meeting house (used for both civil and ecclesiastical meetings) there was no great hardship in the inhabitants of such a town going to one place of meeting, or having one set of constables, or sending their children to one school. But, when for whatever cause, a settlement had grown up at some distance from the centre of the town, then it often became inconvenient, and sometimes dangerous[2] for many of the inhabitants of a town to go to meeting, and it must be remembered that there was often a fine incurred by not being present at town meeting and worse than a fine by absence from divine worship. In such cases the settlement was erected into a district, precinct or parish. The origin of the word district is to be found either in the system adopted for education, or for purposes of taxation. Precinct was the legal term for the bounds of a constable, and parish was borrowed from the English law. The secular affairs of such a settlement after it had

---

[1] Ecclesiastical Law, p. 17.
[2] See Judd's Hist. of Hadley on this point.

been set off were carried on by the inhabitants through by-laws passed at precinct, parish or district meetings, apparently without the medium of selectmen. In ecclesiastical matters it formed a distinct parish or church, it being provided: "That in all such towns where there are or shall hereafter be one or more districts or precincts regularly set off, the *remaining part of such town* shall be and ARE hereby deemed, declared and constituted an entire perfect district, *parish* or precinct, and the *first* or principal of said town."[1] This plainly indicates the origin of "First Parish-church," that is the church of the First Parish or the people who worshipped in the old meeting house. When a district or precinct attained sufficient strength it was incorporated as a town.

The Massachusetts town in 1765 was the political unit. Each town sent one or more representatives to the General Court, had its own church organization, its own military company, its own court for petty causes and made by-laws for the carrying on of its prudential and municipal affairs. The representatives to General Court were elected at a special meeting at which the selectmen presided.[2] At these meetings all persons who owned land of the annual value of 40s., or other property to the amount of 10£ had a vote. As to the election of the town officers proper, the following seems to have been the arrangement in 1765.[3] A regular town meeting was held in March of each year, to which all freeholders rated over £20 could come and vote, and, "by the major vote of such assembly, then and there shall choose 3, 5, or 7 persons . . . . inhabiting within said town to be *selectmen* or townsmen and overseers of the poor when other persons shall not be particularly chosen to that office," and also "town clerk, commissioner for assessments," constables, surveyors of highways, tithingmen, fence viewers, clerks of the market, and other ordinary town officers. Besides these routine meetings

---

[1] Acts and Laws, edition of 1759, page 198.
[2] Ibid., p. 190.
[3] Acts and Laws, ed. 1759, p. 19.

the selectmen upon the written request of ten freeholders of the town were obliged to call a town meeting for the consideration of such business as was mentioned in the request.[1] If the selectmen refused, the constable summoned a town meeting upon the order of a justice of the peace, who, it would seem, was obliged to give the order as a matter of form if requested to do so.[2] At these town or parish meetings order was preserved by a *moderator* elected by those present,[3] and whatever business had been mentioned in the warrant might there be discussed and concluded, and the action of the majority of the qualified freeholders there present was binding upon the town, and upon all the inhabitants thereof.

It seems to have been the custom in the early time and it certainly was the law in 1768, that " the selectmen having instruction in writing from the town may make such necessary rules, orders and by-laws for managing the prudential affairs of the town, not repugnant to Province laws, and to annex penalties not to exceed 20s." " Such orders and by-laws to be binding on being approved by the court of quarter sessions." This reference to the quarter sessions dates as far back as 1692, and probably farther. The delegation of authority to the selectmen, as described above, is a good example of the nature of their office. The town possessed the power to do pretty much as it pleased with regard to its own affairs, and the selectmen, unless their action was overruled, possessed an almost equal amount of authority. In small towns in addition to their regular duties they performed those belonging to the office of town treasurer, overseer of the poor, board of health, assessors, and school committee.[4] As selectmen[5] they presided at meetings for the

---

[1] Acts and Law, ed. 1759, p. 190.

[2] Ibid., p. 22.

[3] Ibid., p. 189.

[4] Acts and Laws, ed. 1759, p. 19.

[5] For Selectmen's Duty and Power, see Table to Laws of 1660, ed. of 1672, under " Townships ; " " County and Town Officer " and " Province Laws ; " Laws of 1759, Table under " Select-men."

election of representative, and decided disputes " at *town* or
parish meetings, about the qualification of voters, before the
moderator is chosen," and they also approved of new inhabitants and had many other minor duties.

The officer next in importance was the constable,[1] who was
elected at the regular March meetings, and who warned all
town meetings when so ordered by the proper authority.   In
the smaller towns, he acted as tax collector, and as such, if
the selectmen neglected to make a rate for the support of the
ministers, the constables, upon the order of two justices of
the peace (one being of the *quorum*), were obliged to collect
the rate and pay it over.   As to his regular duties he performed those of the constable and beadle of old England, with
the exception that in Massachusetts there seems to have been
no provision made for raising the hue and cry, save in the
early time.

The surveyor[2] of the highways was chosen at the March
meeting. He had charge of "highways, private ways, causeys,
and bridges;" and had power to cut down, dig up or remove
anything "that incommoded highways," "as also to dig for
stone, gravel, clay, marl, sand or earth in any land not planted
or enclosed, and to *press* carriages, workmen or other things
fit to be employed in highways." As to the labor necessary,
"surveyors shall appoint the days, provide materials for
working on the highways according to the season of the year
and weather and give public notice thereof; and all persons
from sixteen years old and upward, by themselves or others
in their stead shall attend; or with cart and team, as they
shall be appointed," etc.[3]

The overseers of the poor, assessors and collectors of taxes
performed the duties usual to such officers, with the excep-

[1] Comp. authorities above cited under "constable" with Duke's Laws in
the first Vol. of the Coll. of N. Y. Hist. Soc.

[2] U. S. under Highways and Surveyors.

[3] Comp. p. 20 *et seq.*, for the English custom, and p. 45 *et seq.*, for the Virginia custom.

tion of the collector who seems to have had power to seize upon the persons of delinquent tax payers and to commit such to prison without any further warrant.

The town clerk was the counterpart of the vestry clerk of old England, in that he was the recorder of all town votes, grants, etc., and also the orders of the selectmen. In addition, however, he acted as registrar of births, marriages, deaths, etc.; granted replevins, summonses, attachments for matters triable before a single justice, and summonses for witnesses not only to such trials, but also in civil causes " at the superior and inferior courts."

Fenceviewers were to take care that fences were four feet high, of reasonable strength, and in a good state of repair; and they had considerable authority as to the carrying into execution of their orders. The hayward in England was the watcher of bounds, but his office in Massachusetts, resembled that of the impounder and common driver more than it did that of the hedge warden of the mother country. The tithingmen and wardens of Massachusetts performed certain duties which in old England were attached to the offices of churchwardens and synodsmen. They saw to the observance of the laws against cruelty to animals, tippling and selling strong drink without license, and in general to the "observation of the laws against drunkenness, prophaness and other immoralities." They were required to inform of breaches of the laws, and in fact of anything that seemed to be against the ideas of morality and decency that then prevailed. Before 1756–57,[1] the jurors for both the grand and petty juries were elected at town meetings, but after that time a system of drawing by lot,[2] very like that now in vogue, was adopted.

The old county court disappeared with the colonial charter, and in its place appeared two courts, one for civil causes,

---

[1] Province Laws, III., 474.
[2] Province Laws, III., 995.

called the Inferior Court of Common Pleas, which was held
by four justices appointed for the purpose; and one for criminal offences called the Quarter Session of the Peace, presided
over by the justices of the peace for the county, each of
whom had power within his county to determine civil causes
under 40s.[1]

In 1697, the name Quarter Sessions was changed to
General Sessions; and as the Court of Common Pleas seems
never to have been held in much esteem by the people, the
General Sessions took the place of the old County Court in
the political organization. This court decided what highways were *advisable* and appointed a committee of freeholders
to decide upon the *necessity* or *convenience* of the same; if
their decision was favorable, the sheriff summoned a jury to
lay out the highway and to assess and decide *all questions* of
"*dammages.*" In later times five freeholders were appointed
to lay out the highway, the jury merely estimating the damages. After the way was laid out each town built and kept
in repair such portions as lay within the town limits. The
Court of General Sessions granted licenses to innholders,
liquor sellers, and keepers of coffee houses. It licensed the
erection of fish wears, approved town by-laws, and in certain
cases saw to the relief of the poor.

The justices in each year decided what sums of money were
necessary to defray these and other county charges and the
amount so determined was apportioned among the several
towns according to the rate of the Province levy. The selectmen, or assessors if there were any, assessed the levy and it
was collected as were the town taxes. The Court of General
Sessions seems to have had the absolute disposal of the sums
so raised.

The ministerial officer of the county was the sheriff. He
was appointed by the governor, had custody of the county
jail, served precepts on selectmen in the matter of the choice

---

[1] Province Laws, I., 72–248, 283 and 368.

of representatives, had certain duties in the collection of the county tax, and, in general, performed the duties which belonged to the office of sheriff. Such was the local government of Massachusetts in 1765.

Local Government in Virginia.

In 1769, the local government of Virginia was based upon the county, the parish and the precinct. With the exception of the last of these divisions, size had little to do with their name, for some counties contained many parishes, while on the other hand some parishes comprised more than one county.[1] As to the origin of these divisions, there is little known beyond the bare facts to be given in the next few pages, but in all probability there was less system in the planting of Virginia than there was in the settlement of New England. While in some parts of the colony a newly settled portion became a county and parish at one and the same time, in other regions the hostility of the natives, or some other reason, made it convenient for every little settlement or plantation to have its own house of worship. Thus it came about that in the early days plantation, congregation, hundred, parish, and city were nearly synonymous terms.[2]

To the first General Assembly (1619) there came burgesses from "James City," "Captain Ward's Plantation," and nine other places;[3] but according to "The list of the living on February 16, 1623,"[4] the colony then contained twenty-four

[1] Jefferson's Notes, 148, ed. Boston, 1802. As to the sizes of parishes "the incumbent of the parish [Bristol] reported to the Bishop of London in 1724, that his cure was 40 miles long and 25 miles wide." Slaughter's History of Bristol Parish, p. XVI. and 9. Bristol parish at one time appears to have contained five churches and two chapels.

[2] Meade, Vol. I., p. 238 and 239.

[3] Colonial Records of Va., Richmond, 1874, p. 9; Neill, 139. In Rolfe's Relation, Neill, 107, are the names of the places settled in 1616. See also Hamor's True Discourse, p. 31–32, ed. of 1860.

[4] Colonial Records of Va., p. 37.

settlements, the names of which do not correspond with those given in "a list of those who perished in the massacre of 1622.[1] In 1629, according to a list of the burgesses elected to the Assembly[2] of that year, twenty-four places or plantations enjoyed the right of representation in that body ; but before the next Assembly (1631 O. S.), the plantations were consolidated, and to it came burgesses from only thirteen places. This list[3] of 1631 is important because it is the first in which we find the word parish—" Waters Creek and the upper parrish of Elizabeth City." This is not, however, the first time that the word parish occurs in the records, because, as far back as 1623, we find it in " Hening," and the word churchwarden is in the " Laws of 1621 ;"[4] but this, of itself, does not necessarily imply that there were parishes organized at that time. Indeed, as late as 1627, we read of the " Minister and churchwardens of 'Stanley Hundred ;' "[5] and, therefore, as this return of a burgess from the Upper Parish of Elizabeth City is the first mention of the parish as a living organization, we may date its appearance in official documents at 1631.[6] Now, what was the early history of the county ?

In 1618, the Governor and Council had been ordered to divide the colony into counties,[7] but there is no reason to suppose that they did so ; for, five years later, among the " First Laws," so-called, is the following : " that they shall be courts [of record] kept once a month in the corporation of Charles City and Elizabeth City, ... that the commanders of the places and such others as the governor and

---

[1] Neill, p. 339.

[2] Hening, Vol. I., p. 138.

[3] Hening, Vol. I., p. 153.

[4] Hening, Vol. I., p. 122; Ibid., p. 125, contain something of interest in the history of religion in the colony.

[5] Hening, Vol. I., p. 145, note.

[6] A list of the parishes in 1680, is in the Colonial Records of Va., p. 103.

[7] In Hening, I., p. 115, the words are " Cities, boroughs, etc.," but the Rev. P. Slaughter gives the words as in the text, with the exception of the word " ordered," in his History of Bristol Parish, 2d ed., p. 4.

council shall appoint by commission shall be the judges, with reservation of appeal after sentence to the governor and council . . . . The commanders to be of the *quorum* and sentence to be given by the major parties."[1] In 1628–9, the words[2] "Monthly Courts" occur and they appear again in 1631–32.[3] At last in 1634, we come upon the following: "Roll, No. 11, 1634. Pa. 174—Sheriffs appointed for the several counties:"[4] and in that year the colony was divided into eight shires which were to be governed like the English shires, with "lieutenants" and sheriffs and "*sergeants*, and *bailiffs* where need requires." The commissioner of the Monthly Court was to have cognizance of 10£ instead of 5£ causes, and one of the council was to sit with him. The date of the county then is 1634. In 1642, there were ten counties, and among the laws enacted that year is the following: "that the said monthly courts be reduced to six yearly, ... and instead of monthly courts to be called countie courts, and the commissioners to be styled Commissioners of the Countie Courts."[5] These officers were called justices of the peace in 1661, when the monthly sittings of the courts were resumed.[6]

The county was a territorial division, the inhabitants of which belonged to one body of militia, commanded by a county lieutenant; and between whom justice was administered by eight or more gentlemen, sitting as a county court.

The county lieutenant, who corresponded to the Lord Lieutenant of England, was always one of the most important men of the county, and received his appointment from the governor and council. He commanded the militia of the county, and

---

[1] Hening, Vol. I., p. 125.
[2] Hening, Vol. I., p. 133.
[3] Hening, Vol. I., pp. 163 and 168.
[4] Hening, Vol. I., pp. 223, 224. There is a hiatus from this entry to 1642, except an entry under date of 1639.
[5] The assembly at this sitting made what amounted to a codification of the laws; Hening, Vol. I., pp. 239, *et seq.*
[6] Hening, II. 69; Present State, p. 43.

had authority to "list all male persons above the age of eigh-
teen years . . . . under the command of such captains as he
shall think fit." He could order private drills whenever he
pleased, and was obliged to hold a general muster four times
a year. He presided at court-martials, and had considerable
dictatorial power in time of war.

In 1769 the county court was held monthly at places ascertained by law. It consisted of eight or more gentlemen,
inhabitants of the county, commissioned by the governor,[1] and
called justices of the peace, four of whom, one being of the
"*quorum*," constituted a court. These courts had cognizance[2] "of all causes whatsoever at the Common Law or in
Chancery within their respective jurisdictions, provided the
amount in dispute was over 25 shillings and that the penalty
for the alleged crime was not loss of life or member, or out-
lawry."[3] Matters under 25 shillings were determined by a
single justice, while all greater crimes were adjudicated by the
Governor and council in what was called the *General Court.*
Besides its judicial functions the county court had authority[4]
to erect and keep in repair the County Court House. It had
sole charge of highways, (causeys), bridges, "*churchroads*,"
etc., could contract for the construction of a bridge or road,
and, if no contract was made, procured labor as follows: the
whole county was divided into precincts or "walks" of a
suitable size, in each of which a "surveyor"[5] was appointed.
The court decided when the work should be done, and at that
time every tithable[6] male was required to labor under the
direction of the surveyor, who seems to have been a mere
foreman; the only exemption from this service was, that any
person who owned two or more tithable slaves was not com-

---

[1] Hening, V. 489.   See Beverly, 203, who says Governor and Council.
[2] For the jurisdiction of this court in early times see Hening, Vol. I., p. 163.
[3] Hening, V. 491.
[4] Hening, V., p. 507.
[5] Beverley, ed. of 1722, p. 208 ; Hening, II. 103, for Act of 1661.
[6] For tithable, see p. 50.

pelled to serve in person, but, nevertheless, was required to send such slaves.[1]

The county court could clear rivers of obstructions, and had certain powers with regard to water mills. It ordered the processioning of the parishes, licensed taverns,[2] recommended inspectors of tobacco, designated places for tobacco warehouses and "landings," and probably appointed constables. Each year the court presented the names of three of its members to the governor, who appointed one, generally the senior justice, to be sheriff of the county for the ensuing year.

The sheriff was the ministerial officer of the county court, and as such performed the duties belonging to that office as they are described in Dalton's *Officium Vice Comitum*, (a copy of which was ordered to be purchased in 1666), so far as such description was applicable to Virginia.[3] Besides these duties he collected the "quit rents," the public and county levies, and usually the parish levy. He held the election for burgesses and summoned both grand and petty juries for the county and General Courts.[4] Trial by jury seems to have been given the colony by the "Company" in 1621, and to have been confirmed by the Act of 1642; but beyond the mere mention of them and their qualifications I have found nothing concerning the petty juries at the county court. The juries which tried the capital offences at General Court (session of oyer and terminer) were summoned from the county in which the crime was alleged to have been committed, but if the accused challenged any of these, their places were filled from the bystanders.[5]

---

[1] It is interesting here to note that according to the law of 1657, the county court, in laying out roads, etc., was to pay regard to the "course used in England," Hening, I., 436.

[2] Hening, I., 411.

[3] Hening, Vol. II., p. 246. See also Act of 1748—Hening, V., 515, 552. "Laws" of 1754 and "Laws" of 1769.

[4] See Hening, V., 525, 526; and Laws in Force in 1769, p. 189. Also Laws of 1728, p. 275.

[5] The Acts of Assembly now in Force, Williamsburg, 1769, p. 200, (cited here as Laws in Force, 1769.

So that the jury of the vicinage, in our sense of the term, can scarcely be said to have existed in the Old Dominion. The sheriff seems to have been assisted by an officer called the Constable.

According to Beverley[1] "Constables are appointed, relieved and altered annually by the county courts as they see occasion, and such bounds are given them as those courts think most convenient.[2] These "bounds" were called precincts, but I have been unable to find either in "Hening" or in any of the numerous collections of the laws of Virginia, anything confirmatory or otherwise of this description from Beverley. The Constable, besides having co-ordinate authority with the sheriff, in many cases, had considerable authority of his own. He collected fines for small offences, whipped criminals who could not pay, arrested violators of the revenue laws, and accompanied those who searched suspected places for smuggled goods or the houses of papists for arms, horses, etc., and he had sole charge of runaways whether sailors, servants or slaves. In addition he had the duty peculiar to Virginia of making "perambulations"—so-called—to view tobacco fields, and to destroy inferior growths as "suckers" and "seconds." He executed the game laws and, as part of this duty, he visited in his "perambulations" the negro quarters, and killed any dogs above the number of two there found. He had other minor duties as will appear by the following table of fees:[3]

		Pounds of tobacco
"For serving a warrant - - - -		10
" summoning a witness - - - -		5
" " a coroner's jury and witnesses -		50
" putting into stocks - - - -		10
For whipping a servant or slave - - -		10
For removing any person suspected to become chargeable to the parish; to be paid by the parish for every mile going and returning - - -		2."

[1] Ed. of 1722, p. 215.
[2] Ibid., p. 208.
[3] Hening, V., p. 340.

This compensation was further increased by one pound of tobacco out of the county levy for each "tithable" in his precinct, and, besides, he received many fees not above enumerated, and was exempt from jury service and from the payment of taxes while in office. If we should suppose that the precincts of the constable and surveyor corresponded in extent to the parish, and that the parish and county were— as in many instances was the case—the same, we should have all the duties performed by a New England town under one government.

The parish was, as a rule, a division of the county for religious purposes; but the governing body of the parish, the vestry, had considerable authority in civil affairs. The first mention of vestry in "Hening"[1] is in 1642-3; namely, "That there be a vestry held in each parish for the making of the levies and assessments for such uses as are requisite and necessary for the repairing of the churches," etc. And that there be yearly chosen two or more churchwardens in every parish. " That the most sufficient and selected men be chosen and joined to the minister and churchwardens to be of that vestry." This law was probably a mere codification of the existing usage, for it will be remembered that churchwardens are mentioned in the "Laws of 1623," and the vestry meant in this act was probably an *open* vestry or, perhaps, a *"committee of assistance"* as above described, for according to a law[2] passed in February, 1644-5, the election of the vestry was in the power of the major part of the parishioners.

But in 1661–62, it was enacted that: "In case of the death of any vestry man, or his departure out of the parish, that the

---

[1] Hening, Vol. I., p. 240.
[2] Hening, Vol. I., p. 290. See also for the early vestry, "Present State," by Hartwell, Blair and Chilton. Lond., 1727. See also Act of 1660–61, Hening, II., 25.

said minister and vestry make choice of another to supply his
room;"[1] and this was law in 1769.[2]

The Virginia vestry held a very unique place in the local
system, for, besides electing churchwardens, presenting ministers to the governor for induction, providing glebes, "parson
houses," and salaries, the vestry had, together with the churchwardens, charge of the poor, the processioning of the parish
bounds,[3] counting tobacco, and many minor duties.

In the Old Dominion there were neither patrons nor
bishops. The governor took the place of the " Ordinary ; "
the county court, of the " Visitation," and the vestry of the
patron. The vestry hired the minister by the year, and for
this reason, and because of low salaries and onerous conditions attached to the holding of the cure, it was very difficult
to get men of ability to stay in the colony for any length of
time. The churchwardens made their presentments to the
county court, not, however, to the prejudice of the grand jury,
which, indeed, often presented the same offences.

There were no overseers of the poor in Virginia, their
duties being performed by the vestry and churchwardens.
In early times the poor were distributed among the planters
of the parish, but in later days a system of workhouses was
introduced which is said to have been profitable to the community.

For the better levying[4] and collecting funds for county
and parochial needs, each county was divided into a suitable

---

[1] For the duties of the vestry, see Meade, I., 364; 394, 395; Slaughter's
Bristol Parish, XIV.–XIX.; Hening, Vol. I., p. 433, for the act of 1657;
History of Augusta County, p. 97; Vestry Book of Henrico Parish, 1730–
1773, edited by R. A. Brock, in Wynne's Historical Documents from the
Old Dominion.

[2] Laws in Force in 1769, p. 2, and Hening, II., 44.

[3] Slaughter, Bristol Parish, p. XVIII. and 11.

[4] The first levy is described in Hening, I., 143. The law of 1646 is in
Hening, Vol. I., p. 329. See also Ib., 342 and 354; Beverley, edition of
1722, pp. 218–219; Present State, p. 53. See for law of 1660, Hening,
II., 19.

4

number of precincts. To each precinct a justice was detailed to whom, on the first day of June in each year, every " head of a family " was to bring in a list of all the persons in his family (including servants and slaves) over the age of sixteen—white women alone excepted—each and every person so reported was a " TITHABLE."

In order to lay the parish levy,[1] the vestry of each parish met in December of each year, and made a computation of the parish debts. The sum thus ascertained was divided by the number of " tithables " in the parish, and the quotient was what each tithable had to pay to the parish. The head of a family paid the amount due from the members of his family, which included his servants and slaves, to the collector, who liquidated the parish debts.

The county levy[2] was laid in the same manner and usually collected by the same officer. If we may believe the author of an article on Truro parish in " Scribner's,"[3] the affairs of the parish were transacted in a business-like way. I have been unable to find a county levy, but the following parish levy will be of interest :

"At the meeting of the 22d of August, 1748, the vestry proceeded to lay the parish levy as follows:[4]

Augusta Parish. Dr.

To the Rev. John Hindman 16,000 lbs. tobacco at 3 farthings per pound without any deduction	£50.	0. 0
To $^{10}/_{00}$ on ditto for collection - - -	5.	0. 0
To Mr. Hindman for board - - -	20.	0. 0
To Sam Says per agreement with churchwardens	1.	4. 0
To James Portees - - - -	2.	5. 0
To Robert McClenachan, per acct. - -	4.	15. 7
To Daniel Harrison, per acct. - - -		10. 0
To John Madison, clerk - - -	8.	0. 0
	£91.	14. 7

---

[1] Beverley and " Present State," as above.

[2] Beverley, 218; " Present State," 53.

[3] Scribner's, XI., 629.

[4] History of Augusta County, p. 99. This is an exact copy of the account there given.

The Parish. Dr.

To the above creditors - - - ·	£91. 14. 7
" deposit in collector's hands - - -	50. 6. 5
	142. 1. 0

Per contra. Creditor.

To 1,421 tithable at 2 s. per pole - -	142. 1. 0."

Shortly after this John Madison was turned out, as he " was not very strict in his accounts."

Another duty of the vestry was the processioning of the bounds of every person's land, which is described as follows.[1] Every fourth year upon the order of the county court, the vestry divided the parish into precincts of convenient size, and appointed " two intelligent, honest freeholders of each precinct," to see that such processioning was performed, " and who should take and return to the vestry an account of every person's land they shall procession and of the persons present at the same time and what lands," etc. These reports were registered by the parish clerk, and this, which corresponded in part to the perambulations of England, was the only method of recording land-titles in Virginia before the Revolution.

The churchwardens were the executive officers of the parish. They were two in number, and were elected yearly by the vestry from among its own number. In speaking of the vestry, I have sufficiently described the office of churchwardens. It only remains to be added that they had the duty peculiar to Virginia, of arresting and selling negroes " unwarrantably " set free.

To sum up, in a county which contained but one parish the local government was in the hands of eight men, appointed by the governor, who administered justice ; of twelve men, except in the early days, elected by their predecessors, (a close corporation), who took care of the poor and had charge of all

---

[1] Laws in Force in 1769, p. 153. Slaughter's Bristol Parish, p. XVIII.

matters pertaining to religion ; and of one man appointed by the governor, who was the head of the military. The two boards first named had power to raise and expend whatever sums of money they saw fit, and, as there was nothing to prevent a man from being at one and the same time county lieutenant, justice of the peace, and vestryman, it might very well happen that all local authority would be centered in the hands of twelve persons, none of whom were elected by the people. In fact, the poor white, except once in a while when he cast a vote for burgess, had no more share in the government than the blackest negro, and, therefore, when the conditions under which this system had grown and flourished were changed, there was no large body of men trained to habits of local self-government as in New England.

The far seeing men of the colony had attempted to counteract the forces which produced this result, as the following extracts show : " December, 1662. Whereas oftentimes some small inconveniences happen in the respective counties and parishes which cannot well be concluded in a general law, Be it therefore enacted, that the respective counties and the several parishes in those counties shall have liberty to make laws for themselves, and those that are so constituted by the major part of the said counties or parishes to be binding upon them as fully as any other act." [1]

In 1676 an attempt was made to have the parish levies laid by the " vestry and six sober, discreet housekeepers or freeholders," [2] who should sit with them and who were to have been elected by the freeholders of the parish. This was not taken advantage of by those whom it was supposed to benefit. Neither did the act above quoted work well, for in 1679 it was declared that the former act was too general, and it was therefore enacted that for the future " two men shall be elected by the parishioners of each parish, who should sit in the

---

[1] Hening, II., p. 171.
[2] Hening, II., 396.

county court and have equal votes with the several justices in the making by-laws."[1]   But this scheme appears to have worked no better.

In 1655–56 it was attempted to make the parish the basis of representation in the assembly, every freeman to have a vote.[2]   In 1699 this last was changed to freeholder, and in 1705 the county was again made the basis of representation. But these laws were not taken advantage of, partly no doubt on account of the extra expense involved, and partly because the genius of the country pointed in another direction.   Such was local government in Virginia in 1769.

CONCLUSION.

Whoever has followed me thus far must have been impressed with the fact that town and county government in the English colonies were not so unlike as is commonly supposed; that they were *both* the survival of the English common law parish of 1600; and that the difference, such as it is, in these forms may be traced to the causes above described.

The constitutional history of Massachusetts and Virginia before their settlement is one history—the continuous history of the English people.   Both colonies were founded by commercial companies.   New England's plantation and Bermuda Hundreds were very similar; while Captain Ward's "particular plantation" in Virginia was a good example of what Matthew Cradock's farm and "park" were to have become in Massachusetts.   The Virginia Company lost its charter and the colony became a royal province, while the government of the colony planted by the Company of Massachusetts Bay, owing to the removal of the charter to America,

---

[1] Hening, II., p 441.

[2] Lynnhaven parish was given the right to choose burgesses in 1642; Hening, I., 2.   See also Hening, Vol. I., p. 277; Ib., p. 421.   Ib., Vol. I., pp. 469, 476, for Acts of 1657–8.

became, at least so far as the freemen of the corporation were concerned, almost democratic.   And this was perfectly natural, for, while Virginia was settled on account of the wealth to be gained from a successful cultivation of her soil, the early colonists of Massachusetts were men and women to whom wealth, except as an accompaniment of a pure and decent life, was no recommendation.   It was to attain that purity of social life that they left comfortable homes in England to subdue the wilderness of the New World.   Consequently, while the plantations of Virginia became more and more dispersed, those of Massachusetts grew up side by side, each little collection of plantations forming a town.   Then an ecclesiastical organization, in each case congenial to the respective social conditions was introduced; and lastly, a mode of land distribution most favorable to the successful carrying out of the objects for which the respective colonies were founded was devised for each colony.

In the Old Dominion and in Massachusetts the county was the offspring of the " city " (Va.) and plantation.   In the northern colony the town, which was but the successor of the plantation, remained as the basis of the social organization; while in the southern colony the municipal division entirely disappeared and the parish filled the vacancy as well as it could.

The English parish was " *locus quo populus alicujus ecclesiæ degit;* " or the " multitude of neighbors pertaining to one church; "[1] and, if we were in want of a definition of an early Virginia parish or an early New England town, no words could be found to better express the *thing*.[2]

The " assistance " of the parish, by English common law became in time the select vestry of the England and Virginia of the last century; while in Massachusetts the " survival "

---

[1] Minsheu, Guide into the Tongues, p. 348.
[2] Note especially the use of the word " body " in the early records of Dorchester and other New England towns.

of the "assistance"—the "select persons" (five men, ten men, townsmen, or selectmen)—was never permitted to turn into a close corporation and become permanent. This is the point, for the select men of New England, *while in office,* possessed very nearly the power the select vestry exercised. Various institutional analogies will be clearly seen in the following tabulated statement of the powers of the local organization in

(1) ENGLAND.	(2) MASSACHUSETTS.	(3) VIRGINIA.
Parish or *Town.*	*Town.*	*Parish.*

Powers exercised in

Parish Meeting.	*Town Meeting.*	*Vestry Meeting.*

By

Parishioners.	*Inhabitants* thro' By-Laws or certain officers.	*Vestrymen.*
Assistance and *Churchwardens.*	*Selectmen* and *Ruling Elders.*	*Vestry* and *Churchwardens.*

The powers thus exercised were, in ecclesiastical matters, exercised as follows:

Ministers appointed by

Patron.	*Congregation* (*Town*).	*Vestry.*

And paid by

Tithes, etc.	*Congregation* (*Town*).	*Vestry.*

The goods used in the conduct of divine service being in the hands of

Churchwardens (responsible to *Parish*).	*Congregation* (*Town*).	*Churchwardens* (responsible to *Vestry*).

Necessary Money raised by

Parish (*Church Rate*).	*Town.*	*Vestry.*

In Military Organization the basis was the

Parish.	*Town.*	*County.*

The charge of the Poor was in hands of the

Parish.	*Town.*	*Vestry.*

Which exercised this duty through the

Overseers of the Poor. (*Churchwardens*, *ex-officio*, being two.)	*Overseers of the Poor*, (if none were elected, the *Selectmen*).	*Churchwardens* and *Vestry.*

The funds required for the Poor were raised by

Parish.	*Town.*	*Vestry.*

The Highways were laid out by authority of

County.	*County Court* (in first instance, actually by 5 *Freeholders*).	*County Court.*

Highways were built by

Parish.	*Town.*	*County.*

Every male over a certain age was required to work, under the supervision of a Surveyor, chosen by the

Parish.	*Town.*	*County Court.*

The Police Officer was the Constable elected in the

Leet (or otherwise).	*Town Meeting.*	*County Court.*

Funds for purely local needs were voted by

Parish. (Parish Meeting).	*Town.* (Town Meeting).	*Vestry.* (Vestry Meeting).

" Inhabitants " were admitted or refused by

| *Parish.* | *Town* (in Town Meeting *or* thro' the *Selectmen*). | *Vestry.* |

Thus we might go on to the end of the list. With the exception of the charge of the building and repairing of the highways, we may say with truth that the local government of Virginia was in the hands of a body of men originally chosen by the people, but which, in course of time, hardened into a close corporation ; while in Massachusetts the control of local affairs was in the hands of the people, whose agents were the selectmen. And it is possible, therefore, to apply to her institutions the words of Sir Thomas Erskine May used in describing the England of bygone days : " Thousands of small communities there enjoyed the privilege of self-government, taxing themselves through their representatives, for local objects : meeting for discussion and business; and animated by local rivalries and ambitions." It is as true of Virginia as it is of England, that " this popular principle [the right to meet in parish meeting, etc.] gradually fell into disuse; and a few inhabitants,—self-elected and irresponsible,—claimed the right of imposing taxes, administering the parochial funds, and exercising all local authority. This usurpation, long acquiesced in, grew into a custom . . . . The people had forfeited their rights and select vestries ruled in their behalf."

4

9 780788 442681